STUTTERING, IT'S WHAT YOU THINK:

A GUIDE ON SPLIT-SECOND DECISION MAKING
FOR PARENTS AND PROFESSIONALS WHO LOVE
AND TEACH KIDS WHO STUTTER

DOMINIQUE KENNEDY
GEOFFREY MOUNT VARNER

YVES PUBLISHING

The information and advice contained in this book are based upon the research and the personal and professional experience of the authors. They are not intended as a substitute for consulting with a healthcare professional.

PRINT ISBN: 978-1-7348653-0-1

Manufactured in the United States of America

STUTTERING, IT'S WHAT YOU THINK:

A GUIDE ON SPLIT-SECOND DECISION MAKING FOR PARENTS AND PROFESSIONALS WHO LOVE AND TEACH KIDS WHO STUTTER

CONTENTS

INTRODUCTION

Dear Parent,

I know that it's not always easy. Your measure of patience from one day to the next can, at times, waiver as you weigh what your child may encounter on any given day. You settle your thoughts, knowing that things will be okay or eventually get better. You wonder is, "better" just relative to what you are feeling and experiencing right now. You go from being settled on, "stuttering is possibly here to stay," to mindfulness of the fact that your child is experiencing stuttering and most days taking it in stride. Okay, so you had a good day. You handled the situation well. You didn't interrupt him while he was speaking and provided gentle reminders of speech strategies ("Consider your speech helpers," you'd say patiently). You got through it. But what about those other days?

What about those times when you couldn't take it anymore, so you cut him off justifying it with the fact that he needed to think about his speech strategies? I get it. Those days are not full of our most proud parent moments. Guess what parent. It's okay, you're okay, it's going to be okay. Hang in there. You are stronger than you think, and you are indeed stronger than anything that stuttering would dare to deter in you or your child. You are in the driver's seat. You can steer this vehicle and mobilize yourself with the right equipment to help your child feel confident about his speech and become proficient in his communication skills. That's why you've arrived here, right. We are in this together, and you are on the path to guiding your child toward success. Journey with me as we explore the nature of speech, particularly stuttering and speech.

1

A CHILD'S SPEECH

I dreaded hearing my name called in class, only to be left standing vulnerable and exposed. The mere thought of it brought me so much fear and anxiety. I hated the feeling that I always got in the pit of my stomach when I had to say something out loud in front of a group of people, especially when my words were unplanned and unrehearsed. Rather than the fight or flight response that some people get, the fear itself rendered me frozen and foggy. I was unable to collect my thoughts or piece together what I wanted to say. I stood alone feeling humiliated without anyone to rescue me or help string together the unraveling thoughts and words inside of my head. I was rendered speechless with only a cascading mess of umms and uhhs to shuffle through. The mental replay of stumbling over my words nearly jolted me into a panic attack.

Mostly, I hated not being able to share freely, the one thing that I wished I could have control over when it mattered most--- my words. They must think I'm slow or incapable of standing up to the challenge, or worse, they must think I'm a fraud. Sure, my grades were excellent; in fact, I never saw my first 'C' until *after I'd graduated from high school with honors, but what good are superior grades without a strong voice to back them. "What good is it to be in the top 10% of your class if you can't even deliver a simple speech?" was the thought that regularly flooded my head. I'd reasoned that I couldn't just be great on paper and failure in front of everyone. Honestly, it was a mortifying feeling that I can still feel the sting of when I allow my mind to go back to those dreadful times. Times where I felt like my voice was literally being choked out of me by fear. Times of trembling and sweating through class presentations, but mostly, times of feeling like a defeated failure.*

Instead of compassion and understanding, I got the familiar look of pity. I could always see it in their eyes, at least in the ones that stayed around long enough to watch me fumble over my broken words. It would always start as a rhythmic head nod, almost willing the words to come into alignment. Their eyes would shift with discomfort, straining not to look away too often but painstakingly listening, in search of some glimmer of hope that I would somehow, eventually, get through the disastrous delivery of a speech. Lastly came the look of sympathy as I finally figured out how to struggle to close out the terrifying talk. During those times, I desperately wanted to mop up the mess I'd made of my words and scurry to my seat, attempting with all my might to smile through sullen eyes, sunken shoulders, and a sulky mood.

While I wish that I could say that this is a fictitious story, it is, in fact, a real personal account. Thanks to a great deal of introspection and formalized strategies, it is now a part of my story that I no longer deny but freely admit as a true lived experience and one that so many people across the globe face in their own way, during their own daily walk of life. Thankfully I did find my voice and am now able to support others to find and connect with their own voice.

This book is for you and about your child who stutters. This book is for adults who stutter and want to be the person you needed when you were younger. This book is an instructional tool for parents and professionals who are prepared to place a demand on how stuttering is viewed and how it impacts the people they love.

As a speech-language pathologist, I have the honor of providing help to you, your children and other families, through customized services as a result of not only my specialized training in speech but also my experiences as well. As you dive fully and completely into this book, it is my desire that you see yourself or loved one and therefore empower you to better understand the pain points and triumphs through the lived experiences of others while reflecting on aspects of your own story.

Allow me to share further on how the story of others has impacted me both personally and professionally. It is through these stories that we can thoroughly examine our hearts and minds on this topic as the subject of stuttering is not only a social-emotional journey but also a tangible one. When we can sincerely and unashamedly own our story, we can strategically move forward toward solutions and strategies of success as it relates to stuttering while acknowledging the root issues of speech.

Let me share a story with you about a young man. I will call him Blake. Blake is mild-mannered, inquisitive, and athletic. Blake is a male in his late teens who acquired a severe stutter after what was supposed to be a routine surgery gone terribly wrong. While his mother was concerned and hysterical, he arrived at my office mildly stressed by the recent onset of stuttering. Having been fluent before his injury, Blake now exhibited long blocks (pauses) at the beginning of every other word, which was accompanied by behaviors that would present as odd to most or a medical emergency to others. It was during his first visit that he reflected on his traumatic surgical experience. While he was unable to recall all the events leading up to the onset of his stuttering, he could not erase from his mind what he described as a feeling of deep scraping and excruciating pain during his surgical procedure. Subsequently, what followed the surgery was severe stuttering disorder characterized by lengthy blocks (i.e., pauses), whole word repetitions, part word repetitions, and odd body responses. Demonstrated through untimely eye blinks, hand gestures, and head nods. At seventeen-years-old, this young patient now self-identified as one of roughly 3 million Americans who stutter. If you're inquisitive, like me, and armed with rapid-fire questions, you are likely wondering why and how this could have happened.

So, where do we go when we want answers? Often we can find ourselves scouring the internet to look up some undetermined, unimaginable, inconceivable reason "why' for one thing or another. Searching for answers to figure out," Is this normal? "Why does my child do that? Or "what happens when you? Google has become the gold standard for any and all things to know or DIY (e.g., "diagnose it yourself"). In fact, the most searched or popular keywords on google range from "weather" in the number one spot to "prodigy" in the fifty-sixth spot. Surprisingly the most asked question on Google is "what is my IP" perhaps less surprisingly the sixteenth most asked question is "how to get pregnant" (#52 goes to "how to make love" #91 "how many people are in the world" #99 what is the meaning of life). Why am I mentioning this at all, and how is it relevant to you? My point is that we are all in some way, searching for answers. We are all in some way seeking to define our purpose. In some way, we all need to feel a sense of belonging.

As a person who stutters or as a parent of a child who stutters, belonging, and acceptance might be at the very top of your list as you encounter everyday life and wonder, "Is there anyone else in the world like me." Is there anyone that really gets what it feels like to always be concerned or even fearful of how your words will be perceived when you stutter.   I will share some information in this book on stuttering, and I will provide terms and theories related to stuttering.   It is my goal that you finish this book feeling informed and empowered to do whatever it is that you believe you are supposed to do to make a wonderful life for yourself and for your family, with or without stuttering.

A BOY'S STORY

It was Wednesday morning, and I was sitting in my second-grade reading class. It was time to go around the room, and each student had to read aloud. I had already gone to the bathroom to prevent being called on by the same teacher during the previous social studies class. And I had been to the school nurse too many times already, and it was just October.

I knew that if I had to read aloud, it meant that I was going to have to fight during lunch again and did not feel like it. Let me explain, I am a stutterer and have stuttered since I was able to speak. No, there was not a tragic or traumatic event. As my grandmother used to say, "some people are just made extra special." As a child, I did not want to be special.

Bottom line is, kids can be mean. Back to reading aloud in class. The rule in the class was the person reading could keep reading until they missed or stumbled on a word. You received high praise from the teacher and respect from your fellow 2nd graders if you were able to read 2 - 3 paragraphs.

I could not read more than 2 words before I would stutter. And that is when Billy would start to purposely stutter aloud in *front of the whole class. I still do not know why the teacher was not able to put an end to it. And a lot of the kids would laugh too. A few times when it was Billy's turn to read, he would raise his voice and say, "who am I reading right now," and then begin to purposefully stutter while he was reading.*

Once Billy would purposefully tease me, second-grader unwritten rules meant that I had to say to Billy, "I will see you on the playground." And that meant it was time to fight. I do not know why I would say that each time. Billy was bigger and stronger than me and beat me up most of the time. Except for this one time. Billy came charging at me and knocked me over. We started wrestling, and the teacher came and stopped the fight. On this occasion, when the teacher broke us up, Billy had a bloody lip. Billy's lip had gotten caught on my zipper. And all the kids laughed and joked that I had beat Billy up.

To be clear, I did not fight Billy because I thought I could beat him. But I knew that if I let Billy bully me unhindered, all the other kids would see me as an easy target.

What is the point of this story? As a stutterer, our lives are different. Our stutter singles us out. As a child, that can be sad, scary, and unfortunate. If parents or the caregiver is supportive and protects the child from the mess that adults create, due to stuttering, then the stutter is a blessing.

It is like what the late poet, Douglass Malloch, writes in his poem "Good Timber Does Not Grow on Ease":

"The tree that never had to fight for sun, sky, air or light never became a forest king, but lived and died a common thing. Good timber does not grow on ease. The stronger the winds, the stronger the tree, the more the sky the more the length, the more the storm the more the strength by sun by cold, by rain and by snow in tree or man does good timber grow."

Meaning, as a result of being tested in so many social, emotional, cultural, and educational ways as a result of being a stutterer, you develop additional skills. You create other survival tools. For instance, a lot of stutterers' focus on their math and science skills. And nearly all stutterers' are forced to develop their critical thinking skills.

Let me explain, as a stutterer, each word that you speak comes with the inherent risk of you stuttering. Therefore, the stutterer is continually thinking and deciding how to say things more concisely. A stutterer learns that there are certain words that they are more likely to stutter over. Hence you become very strategic in your use of words. All the above creates the ability to think succinctly and critically.

Additionally, the constant having to make multiple decisions about what to say and how to say it and which words to use makes us tired. We experience decision fatigue.

Decision fatigue is the decline of your ability to make good decisions as a result of the multiple decisions that you must make as the day goes on.

We make about 35,000 decisions every day. Most of those decisions are mundane, like what color shirt to wear, which suit to put on, what to eat for breakfast, etc. But only 70 of those decisions are life-changing or life-altering. It is my assertion that given the number of decisions that a stutterer has to make about which words to use, not use or change mid-sentence that we make thousands more of decisions than people who do not experience disfluency.

Hence, stutters are even more prone to decision fatigue.

Let me explain further; our brain is similar to a muscle. For example, when we physically exercise our muscles at some point, they become tired. And when your muscles become fatigued, they do not function as efficiently. A real-life example would be, marathon runners. Early in the race, their pace is strong, consistent, swift, naturally flowing and effortless. We have all seen footage of marathon runners. As the race progresses and towards the end of the race, the runner's stride is not optimal, inefficient, forceful, graceless, and requires a lot of energy – unless you are a well-trained marathon runner which 98% of the world is not. In short, the marathoner is fatigued and thus less efficient in his or her stride.

The brain functions the same way. Early in the day, your brain is refreshed and has plenty of energy and a great deal of thinking power. It can maximally process, synthesize enormous amounts of information and thus make reasonable and thoughtful decisions.

As the day progresses and as you make more decisions, your brain starts to tire. The brain experiences decision fatigue, which is the decline of your ability to make good decisions as you spend more time mulling over other decisions during the day. The more significant the number of decisions both big and small, the sooner your brain becomes tired and thus function less optimally.

In other words, the more daily decisions you need to make as the day goes on, you become worse at weighing all the options and make educated choices.

There are a few famous people who live and act upon the concept of decision fatigue.

1. Former President Obama – Obama states, "You'll see I wear only gray or blue suits; I'm trying to pare down decisions. I don't want to make decisions about what I'm eating or wearing. Because I have too many other decisions to make..." Obama went on to explain, "the act of making a decision erodes your ability to make later decisions." (Baer, 2014)
2. Mark Zuckerberg – echoed that he must serve a billion people and therefore does not want to waste energy on minor decisions when there are larger

impactful ones he needs to make. Mark wears the same grey t-shirt to trim down the number of smaller decisions that he must make. (Baer, 2015)
3. Steve Jobs – wore the same blue jeans and black turtleneck every single day. He also wanted to limit the number of small decisions that he had to make.

In fact, an Israeli study looking at parole boards showed that convicts who appeared in front of the parole board earlier in the day were 65% more likely to be paroled compared to those who appeared later in the day and charged with similar crimes. The study reinforced the importance and impact of decision fatigue.

Debra Cassens Weiss of the American Bar Association sums the study up well... "the study found that board members were more likely to grant parole at the start of the day and after breaks for food. The problem, researchers said, was "choice overload." When faced with too many decisions, people are more likely to opt for the default choice. In these cases, the default was the denial of parole." Meaning, when faced with too many decisions' later in the day after already having made multiple decisions earlier in the day, the board did not have the energy to weigh all the options. (Weiss, 2011)

There was another great study done at the University of Kent. The study had two groups. One group had to engage with a strenuous computer program for 90 minutes. The other group had to watch a brain-neutral video for 90 minutes. Then both groups had to get on exercise bikes and pedal until they were fatigued enough to stop. Each group could choose their own resistance level.

One hundred percent of the time, the group who was not mentally drained (watched the neutral video) outperformed the mentally drained group. But what was more interesting is, each group chose the same resistance level for the bike ride. What that means is we are not very good at knowing when we are cognitively fatigued. Otherwise, the brain-tired group would have chosen a more natural resistance. (Baer, 2013)

Do you know when you are experiencing brain fatigue? Do you have strategies for preventing brain fatigue? And when brain fatigue occurs, what method(s) do you have in place to assist you during the period of fatigue?

One of the easiest and most common ways to assist with improving and staving off decision fatigue is to be sure that you are well-nourished. If your bloodstream sugar levels are low and thus your energy is low, then it is more likely that your brain level energy levels will not be adequate, and you will, thus, experience fatigue sooner.

What is the point, I would assert that a stutterer experiences decision fatigue much earlier in the day as non-stutters? This information arms us with another data point on ways to prevent or decrease the likelihood of stuttering.

We all hear about mindset. I asked several people what mindset meant. I received several different answers for each person. Many were deep and complicated. Often the conversations progressed to, "can a person's mindset be changed? For the sake of argument, all our comments about mindset will be from the perspective that one's mindset is always evolving and thus can be changed and improved.

Back to the definition of mindset. Albert Einstein once said, "everything should be made as simple as possible, but not simpler." The easy and functional definition of "mindset" that we will use is "a set of beliefs or attitudes about yourself and your abilities." For the sake of this book, your mindset includes the beliefs that you hold about your child or loved one who stutters.

Meaning, if you think your child's stuttering is a genetic flaw or makes him "less than" and is thus going to hold him back in life, then that is the mindset that will be directly and indirectly conveyed to the child who stutters. How you see your loved one who stutters is how the stutterer is going to see himself. And it will influence how the world will see your child who stutters too. Now let's address terms often used when discussing the topic of stuttering.

STRAIGHT TALK ABOUT STUTTERING

I sat in my seat at the massive conference captivated by the speaker's storytelling and candor. Beyond that, I was intrigued by his speaking pattern. It was familiar yet craftily constructed. I listened intently at the cadence and rhythm of his speech and knew instantly what I was certain no one else in the room knew. After the speaker finished addressing the audience and left the stage, I waited in the line of people eager to speak with him about what he had shared. While everyone else asked about ways to elevate their business and services by using his successful framework, I was anxious to learn more about his speech history and confirm what I had suspected from the moment he began speaking. I also wondered if he'd be open to sharing his story on how he managed to deliver such a stellar speech virtually unnoticed by the audience that he appropriately identifies himself as a person with disfluency, specifically stuttering.

What is *fluency*? Fluency is speech that is continuous, smooth, and not effortful. A person with fluent speech speaks without interruptions or frequent breaks in the flow of their message.

What is normal *disfluency?* Disfluency is stuttering that begins during a child's intensive language-learning years and resolves on its own sometimes before puberty. It is considered a *typical* phase of language development. Some children who stutter resolve disfluency without treatment.

What is *stuttering* (also known as stammering)? Stuttering is considered a fluency disorder. Stuttering is talking with continued involuntary repetition of sounds, especially initial consonants. Stuttering may also involve part word repetitions (i.e., He w-w-w-wants a cup), one-syllable word repetitions (i.e., No-no-no thanks), prolonged sounds (i.e., mmmmmmmMac is kind), blocks (i.e. [pause] Happy Birthday).

According to the American Speech-Language-Hearing Association, typical disfluency differs from stuttering in that typical disfluency can be characterized by multisyllabic (i.e., ambulance, elephant) whole word and phrase repetitions (i.e., I want-I want juice please), interjections (i.e., Ahh; Eh) and revisions (i.e., I see-I like the dog). (1997-2020) Unlike stuttering, these features are not significant for physical tension, secondary behaviors, adverse reactions, and are absent from family history. Stuttering, on the other hand, is substantial for sound or syllable repetitions, prolongations, or blocks. It is not uncommon for stuttering to be accompanied by physical tension, secondary behaviors (i.e., foot taps, tongue clicks, eye blinking, etc.), adverse reaction, and avoidance of speaking situations.

Regarding the topic being addressed, family history is noted as a risk factor for stuttering. While research and scholarly publications indicate what we currently known as speech-language pathologists regarding the nature and behaviors surrounding fluency and fluency disorder, science can only offer so much about how stuttering manifests from one child to the next and from primary years to adulthood.

The lens through which one views the world is how they will experience the world and how the world will view them. Hence, the lens a child views themselves, and their speech is most significantly shaped by their parents and their daily caregivers. Regardless of science, it is the parent who is the expert on their child. The parent acts as the primary source of information beyond what a textbook or science journal could provide. The parent has the most accurate account of milestones, successes, strengths, and challenges of the child. It is the parent who creates the climate and culture for how a child views themselves. As a parent of a child who stutters, you must have conversations with your child who stutters about stuttering and their specific speech pattern. Exploring thoughts and feelings with your child about their speech makes what could feel like the big, bad monster appear less scary.

Offering language or deciding on terminology that best suits how your family chooses to talk about stuttering will be the motivator to your child feeling empowered to use his or her voice. As a parent of two young children, gathering information, listening, and offering guidance is my go-to, decision-making move. As a Speech-Language Pathologist, I encourage parents to solve problems with their child. It is an absolute must that parents create and pursue opportunities that empowers their child to feel confident in voicing their own thoughts and ideas. When you, as a parent, allow for interactive feedback with your child, you further establish trust between you and your child and foster a safe space for that child. This act positions you as their number one advocate and support system.

WHAT IS STUTTERING

N ow that you have the facts, let's dispel the most common myths about people who stutter.

Myth: *People who stutter can stop if they really want to; they're just acting nervous or shy.*

Being reserved, introverted, or less talkative is not a cause of stuttering. In nearly every case that I've encountered, people who stutter would readily stop on the spot if they could. Stuttering itself does not discriminate based on gender, age, race, or class.

Myth: *People who stutter are just dumb, slow, and less intelligent than those who don't stutter.*

There is no correlation between stuttering and IQ score or intellect. On the contrary, people who stutter tend to boast of a highly developed vocabulary, namely due to the ability to find a word around a stuttered word. Because of the nature of stuttering, people who stutter can rely on a lengthy lexicon of words when sharing thoughts and ideas. Stuttering is not connected to cognitive ability. A person who stutters is just as capable as a person who is typically fluent.

Myth: *Poor parenting is the reason for that child's stuttering (so shame on you bad mom).*

Bad parenting does not cause stuttering. Stuttering is not the parent's fault, nor is it the child's fault. In many cases being the parent of a child who stutters makes the parent especially protective over and sensitive to mistreatment.

Myth: Stuttering is "contagious"; if a child hears another person stutter, it can cause them to start stuttering.

A person cannot catch stuttering from another person. Several factors are considered to play a role in the onset of stuttering, including family history, neuromuscular development, and environmental factors. The root cause of stuttering continues to be researched.

Myth: *Girls stutter just as much as boys.*

Stuttering more commonly affects boys than girls. Interventions are equally effective, regardless of gender.

Now that we've addressed the misconceptions about stuttering let's consider the straight talk about stuttering.

Fact: *It is not uncommon for children to experience a period of developmental stuttering.*

The incidence of stuttering during early developmental stages is a common occurrence, especially as typically developing young children are acquiring language at a rapid rate. The Stuttering Foundation reports that nearly 5 percent of all children go through a period of developmental stuttering that lasts six months or more. In fact, the majority of those will recover by late childhood.

Fact: *You are not alone as people who stutter live on every part of the globe.*

According to The Stuttering Foundation, more than 70 million people worldwide stutter. In the United States, an estimated 3 million Americans stutter. Support groups and communities, such as the Stuttering and Speech Suite, exist to provide a safe space for people to speak freely and connect with others on stuttering and speech issues.

Fact: *A-list celebrities and famous people stutter too!* People who stutter find success in many professions and industries. The worldwide web can provide lists chock full of celebrities who stutter from Elvis Pressley to James Earl Jones. Our former Vice President of the United States, Joe Biden, also identifies himself as a person who stutters. Don't allow stuttering to stop you or your child from pursuing the purpose that you were set to fulfill.

Fact: *Help is available for people who stutter.* Speech-Language Pathologists are professionals trained to provide assessment and treatment for individuals with communication challenges.

Fact: *Early intervention boasts positive outcomes.* Early intervention services can affect a child's developmental trajectory and increase positive outcomes for children, families, and communities. For early intervention services, visit cdc.gov/FindEI.

Fact: *Resources and support are available for those who stutter.* Organizations and nonprofits exist to provide education and resources for people who stutter. The purpose of this book is to encourage hope and help mindset. It is my desire that parents and professionals utilize this book as a practical resource and support tool for individuals and children who stutter.

REPRESENTATION MATTERS

"... *As a child I felt dumb even though I was one of the smartest in my class. There're lots of issues that kids deal with that stutter.*" *-Johnny Rutledge, NFL veteran*

Unfortunately, there is still a great deal of misinformation related to stuttering. I've had people ask if it is contagious. Others have argued that poor brain wiring is the cause of stuttering. One thing that we can uphold is that stuttering is not limited to one demographic or class of people. Well, known celebrities and notable figures in history are documented as people who stutter. Many highly accomplished individuals identify as people who stutter.

Notably known as the voice of Darth Vader in Star Wars, James Earl Jones is one of the most respected actors in the industry. His voice is recognized as one of the most distinctive in history. In recorded interviews, James Earl Jones describes being silent during a period in his life when stuttering presented as a challenge for him. He also mentions that stuttering is apparent for him when he feels upset, confused, or when competing with outside stimuli rather than tuning to his own thoughts and words. James Earl Jones credits an English teacher for encouraging him to read his own poetry, which he believes contributed to him becoming more proficient in his speaking ability. (Stuttering Foundation of America)

Marilyn Monroe, remembered for her breathy voice and sultry on-screen presence, has documented remarks on her experiences as a person who stutters. "It's painful" are words that Marilyn Monroe used to describe personal hardships and her experience as a person who stutters. (Marilyn Monroe Video Archives, 2011) The throaty vocal quality that she is known for was actually a technique that Monroe adopted after working with a speech therapist to address her difficulties with stuttering. It is reported that Marilyn Monroe was unfortunately fired from her final film, "Something's Gotta Give," due to her difficulty with delivering her lines.

The former vice president of the United States of America, Joe Biden, has brought about an elevated level of awareness for disfluency as he has openly shared his challenges as a person who stutters. Biden reports that for him, stuttering started at age 4. Like many people who stutter, Biden also mentions difficulty with stating his name, making calls primarily via automated systems, and placing orders as people either assume that they are experiencing a poor connection or that he is exhibiting a health issue such as Parkinson's disease. (Brewster, 2020) Joe Biden's political platform has allowed for stuttering to be positioned as a social issue rather than merely an isolated situation.

As an advocate for people who stutter, the more that I connect with people who stutter, the more emphasis is placed on the notion that representation matters. People crave connection with someone that understands. People desperately desire to hear from someone who gets it. That is why representation matters. That's why your child needs to know that they are valued and important. People who are valued go on to add value to others. Your child who stutters needs someone in their corner to remind them that they matter, no matter what! Despite the resonance of their words with others, simply being who they were created to be and facing the world, communicates to your child that their voice matters. While it is not their sole responsibility to educate others about the science of stuttering, sharing their voice with others serves as a conduit for increased awareness and change.

IT'S ITS OWN THING

W e've taken him to every specialist in town, and no one seems to know how to fix this. He has started to hit himself in the throat and say, "I hate my voice, so I'm gonna beat it up for being bad." His father stutters and his grandfather stutters, and I just don't know what to do at this point. It pains me to see him so angry and upset when he can't get his words out. Sometimes he gets so stuck he completely shuts down and decides not to talk at all. He gets this look in his eyes, and he just seems so defeated by this thing that he has such a hard time controlling. I want him to feel in control of what's happening to him. I just want to take the pain away. I'm his mother, I'm supposed to be able to kiss his ouchies away and stop it from hurting him. This, I simply cannot fix or will it away.

As with anything and for some people, there is comfort in categorization and grouping. People generally tend to be tribal in nature. For some people knowing that their situation is less severe than that of another person is comforting. We tend to like to think that my situation is not as bad as so and so situation, or we rationalize that a circumstance is not as far gone as it could be. When getting news from a doctor, for some people, simply putting a name to a set of symptoms brings relief. For others knowing how they are rated on a scale of severity is acceptable. Let's explore the different ways in which people who stutter can be categorized or labeled. The label that is adopted, whether it be difference, disorder, or disability, is your choice. Whether your child's stuttering is very mild or severe, depends largely on the type of stuttering and behaviors being exhibited and clinical judgment. Seek a skilled professional to provide a direct assessment of your child's overall speech and language skills.

When asked by a parent when this "stuttering thing" ends, it is my desire to be clear and direct while acknowledging the immediate status of the person who stutters in consideration of the mindset of the questioner. My answer is that it's subjective because it really depends on several factors. Often awareness, application of strategies, stressors, and factors, both internal and external, can contribute to the severity of a person's incidences of stuttering on any given day. I have found that those who have achieved the greatest level of success include, but not limited to:

(1) overall positive self-concept
(2) supportive environment
(3) connection to community
(4) consistency and commitment to the process.

Having a positive self-concept allows parent and child to view the world and their role in it as impactful rather than detrimental. Your child will make a positive impact in this world, whether stuttering is fully resolved or becomes more easily managed. The way that you view yourself contributes to your actions and decisions. Having a positive outlook and employing positive self-talk will significantly improve how you interact with and respond to others. An overall positive outlook will also allow you to forgive more readily when mistakes or shortcomings occur.

A supportive environment is often a positive indicator when putting a new approach to practice. Some people are built to persevere no matter what the circumstances present. In most cases, having a supportive environment gives a person the will to keep going, especially when things get complicated.

Your connection to your community gives you access to people and services that can significantly benefit your child who stutters. Knowing the best offices to receive skilled speech therapy or being aware of extracurricular activities that will allow your child to shine is of great benefit to your family. Being connected to a community of people who are invested in your child's success is vital to your child's continued progress.

The therapeutic process is one that is unique to each patient and their individual needs, whether your child is receiving services at school or in an office setting. While there are proven interventions that align with what is considered best practices, how your child responds to treatment services, and what strategies work best for him or her is dependent on your child and how they approach services. Committing to speech services, or counseling services if anxiety is a factor, is not only impacting the child but the entire family. Consistency toward the recommended frequency of treatment sessions, carrying out recommended strategies, and ongoing communication with the clinician is critical for progress and change.

As suggested in the chapter on mindset, how a child views themselves as a person who stutters is influenced by the approaches and language that is used by those around the child. Determining how to view and talk about stuttering is a conversation that should include all parties involved. The person who stutters, parents, caregivers, and the education team should all be on board and promoting the same objectives. Even at a young age, a child must know that their voice will be heard in matters concerning their overall communication and speech. Limiting a child's capacity to understand what is happening and how it will be addressed opens the door for questions and potential misconceptions. Include the child as early as possible so that they know that their voice is valuable.

For some parents approaching the conversation on how to talk about stuttering can be daunting, especially if the parent is still working out their own feelings and beliefs about stuttering. Connecting with a community of people is vital when navigating conversations on communication skills and abilities. Here is a list of organizations and resources specific to the needs of individuals and families who stutter.

Empowering your child to be seen and heard-

1. Organizations
2. Stuttering and Speech Suite
3. American Speech-Language-Hearing Association
4. American Board of Fluency and Fluency Disorders
5. National Stuttering Association
6. International Stuttering Association
7. Stuttering Association for the Young
8. Friends: The National Association of Young People Who Stutter
9. Stuttering Home Page
10. StutterTalk

WHAT DO I DO

I keep asking myself when this stuttering thing is going to end! My son has been in speech therapy virtually his whole life, and he's only seven years old. I need someone to tell me that there is an end. I need someone to give me some hope that my son's whole life is not going to be shaped around the fact that he stutters. I keep thinking about what his life is going to be like if this continues. Like if this is really how he will talk for the rest of his life. I keep imagining him as a man, with a job, and a family, and I can't help but wonder how stuttering will affect him. I keep wondering how it will affect my grandkids. I just want to know when it will end. ~ Parent of a seven-year-old boy

Data suggests that early intervention is a predictor of positive learning outcomes. While this is true, stuttering presents with its own unique set of considerations. As discussed in a previous chapter on dispelling myths, it is not uncommon for some children to experience incidences of stuttering during rapid language acquisition stages occurring during early development. In many cases, medical professionals will encourage families to wait for more extended periods of time than necessary to seek specialized help in assessing and addressing communication difficulties. While it is important to maintain a positive outlook rather than succumb to a state of panic, logging observations and seeking the support of a speech-language pathologist to take a closer look at areas of concern for your child is proactive instead of reactive. Some parents choose to wait as the speech difference has not been presented as a concern for the child or family. Indeed, the child must be aware that there is a speech difference to apply fluency modification techniques.

For some parents bringing attention to a child's speech difference implies that it will cause the child to have a complex or negative view of their own speech. As a speech-language pathologist, I encourage early intervention; however, I respect that, beliefs and preferences matter when serving culturally and linguistically diverse individuals and families. It is never my goal to impose my beliefs or bias, rather offer information and allow each person to choose how they will use the information provided. What I do recommend is that parents watch for changes that could influence the social, emotional, or academic status of a child. If frustration, distress, or challenging behaviors are exhibited, then I encourage families to explore reasons as to why the child may be demonstrating the behavior and advise that families rule out environmental or developmental issues. The inability to clearly and concisely communicate thoughts and ideas can be frustrating for any individual, children are not exempt.

8

A HOPE AND HELP MINDSET

As a parent advocate, it is necessary to communicate with your child's teacher to ensure that approaches and considerations are taken into account to best support your child in the classroom but also to provide the teacher with insight on your child as a person. Sample conversation between parent and teacher:

Parent: Hello, Mr. Black. I appreciate you setting up this time to meet with me to discuss our daughter, Blythe.

Teacher: Absolutely! We are thrilled to have Blythe in our classroom. She is such a valuable member of the school community.

Parent: Thanks for sharing. While I know that school has just begun but I wanted to take time to meet with you directly as you may have noticed when speaking with Blythe at the open house that she stutters.

Teacher: I did notice that, so I'm glad that we can discuss it.

Parent: While it is important for us as parents to the teachers and staff that work with Blythe to know that she is a child who stutters, it is also important for her to feel comfortable with speaking up for herself and receiving support as needed.

Teacher: I am more than happy to support Blythe and further educate myself on her individual needs. I have had a child who stutters in my class before and understand that each child is different and how stuttering impacts each child is different.

Parent: Right! We have already begun the work at home by talking about stuttering and ensuring that Blythe is a confident child, and it is our hope that her confidence continues to grow, especially regarding her speech.

Teacher: I agree.

Parent: I know that our conversation has focused on how Blythe's speech, it is also important that you know Blythe's strengths, interests, ambitions, and areas of growth. I have provided more information about Blythe in the form of an "About Me" graphic for your review.

Teacher: Thank you for this!

Some people prepare for the worst but hope for the best. The expression is the glass half-full, or half-empty is a proverbial statement to qualify one's perspective as optimistic or pessimistic. We want so much for our children, and when things arise or do not always go as planned, we must dig deep to employ a glass-half-full perspective. We fear that our child will be hurt. We ponder what-ifs to try to safeguard against every possible negative incident. We are parents and caregivers, so we want to protect our children from harm. Sometimes we push too hard, and we are the ones unknowingly putting our child in harm's way because we wonder what would have happened if someone had pushed us more. We question where we'd be and how far along we'd be if we'd just reach a little farther or push a little harder at a given task.

Sometimes we want to add relief to a situation and simply do not know what to say to mend the hurt or fix the boo-boo. No matter what you are facing with your child who stutters or what next step you may be processing to get them to the next level, trust that you are equipped with everything that you need to be a good parent and provide a meaningful life for your child.   There will be triumphs and challenges as parenting offers many opportunities for teachable moments, both for parent and child. Maintaining a mindset that is positive and set on the truth that your child can be successful is essential.

It's hard as a parent to watch your child stutter and really struggle to get words out.   It is even more difficult when someone challenges your child's intelligence or abilities just because of their speech difference.   It can be equally challenging when someone cuts your child off mid-sentence or tries to finish their statement simply because they want to help them through stuttering, or maybe they are just impatient with your child. It is painful to think back to the times when you, as the parent, were drained from the day or tired and resorted to correcting your child or gesturing to make them hurry through their stuttering. Although you know that you should allow your child to finish out their statement uninterrupted, you just could not bear the thought of them getting stuck and stumbling over their words yet again.

You are not alone. Even parents who stutter admit that conversing with their child who stutters is not always easy even when you know all the right things to do. Be patient with yourself and be patient with your child. Keep in mind that no matter how severe your child's stuttering becomes, it is your job to go to bat for them no matter what. There will be those who will try to mislabel your child or minimize their skill set. It is up to you to build up their confidence so that they can boldly face any obstacle.

9

ADVOCACY

"*P*eople *who stutter are quite a resilient bunch...what other choice do we have?* ~*Ian Mahler*

If I have not emphasized enough, allow me to reiterate that you are your child's biggest advocate and first expert. You know their cry, every facial expression, gesture, preference, mannerism, etc. No one in this world can tell you more about your child than you. While professionals and skilled practitioners have been trained to partner with you on decision making, offer research-based data, and guide certain decisions, at the end of the day, you are the parent. While there are tons of books on parenting, on the job, in the trenches, parenting is a great teacher. That is why partnership and collaboration with your child's teacher are so essential. Teaching the teacher how to best support your child is vitally important. Providing insight to your child's teacher on learning style, interests, and triggers will allow the teacher a more defined lens as to how to best support your child.

Family members also play an important role in the care and considerations that should be discussed concerning your child. Sometimes family members mean well but simply do not have the fundamental understanding of how to approach or talk about stuttering. Some family members may harbor misguided beliefs about people who stutter. Others may not see your child the way that you see them. You may be faced with some difficult decisions as to which family members you will allow in your child's inner circle and which family members must be kept at a distance. Your child's self-confidence and vitality are priority.

Members of the community ought to be included on your child's team. Teams may consist of coaches, family friends, youth leaders, etc. These community members and all those who are invested in your child should be invested in his or her success as it relates to stuttering. Allow community members to support your child as they approach social experiences away from your immediate reach. Allowing community members to support your child who stutters enables your child to build trust and bonds necessary to build their confidence when interacting with peers and unfamiliar adults.

10

LET YOUR VOICE BE HEARD

"*E*verything *will be okay in the end. If it's not okay, it's not the end.*" *John Lennon*

If I leave you with nothing else, it is my hope that I leave you empowered to fight for your child's right to be heard. Be prepared to really fight. Square up! Be in a position to wreak havoc, if absolutely necessary, on behalf of your child. Your child needs you in this war for their voice to be heard. Don't allow fear to choke out your child's voice as it once did mine. Position yourself as a hedge of protection around your child. You are your child's fence. You are the defender of all things bright and wonderful in your child. Parents are to work tirelessly to defend and support the innocence and interests of their child. As your child's advocate, it is essential that they recognize your role as parent and protector.

Parents have the unique ability and responsibility to care for and guide their children toward success. Success, as it relates to speaking situations, does not mean that every speaking situation will turn out perfectly. However, success can mean that your child's voice is acknowledged and heard.

How your child views his or her voice is supported mainly by the love and care that your child receives from you as their parent. So as a parent, you must ask yourself how high is the bar and who placed it there. Is the bar or level of expectation reasonable, regarding your child's speech? Is it fair, given the situation, stage of development, and resources available? As a parent, you must equip yourself with tools so that your child has a full arsenal of resources to rely on. With you as commander-in-chief, along with your child's repertoire of tactics, strategies, and solutions, you equip your child to win the fight, therefore, preparing them for their ultimate success.

REFERENCES

American Speech Language Hearing Association. 1997-2020. Stuttering. https://www.asha.org/public/speech/disorders/stuttering/

Baer, D. (2013, May 14). Quick: End Decision Fatigue Before it Drains Your Productivity Reservoir. *Fast Company*, Leadership Now. Retrieved from https://www.fastcompany.com/3009641/quick-end-decision-fatigue-before-it-drains-your-productivity-reservoir

Baer, D. (2014, Dec. 2). Always Wear the Same Suit: Obama's Presidential Productivity Secrets. *Fast Company*, Work Smart. Retrieved from https://www.fastcompany.com/3026265/always-wear-the-same-suit-obamas-presidential-productivity-secrets

Baer, D. (2015, Apr. 28). The Scientific Reason Why Barack Obama and Mark Zuckerberg Wear the Same Outfit Every Day. *Business Insider*. Retrieved from https://www.

businessinsider.com/barack-obama-mark-zuckerberg-wear-the-
same-outfit-2015-4

Brewster, Jack, 2020, March 19. Joe Biden's Stutter Explains A
Lot About How He Speaks. I Should Know—I Have One Too |
Opinion. Retrieved from https://www.newsweek.com/joe-
bidens-stutter-explains-lot-about-how-he-speaks-i-should-
knowi-have-one-too-opinion-1493176

Marilyn Monroe Video Archives. 2011, June 13. Marilyn
Monroe- I Just Stuttered. Retrieved from https://
youtu.be/zfBJ8HrMZUI.

Stuttering Foundation of America. 1991-2020. James Earl
Jones. https://www.stutteringhelp.org/famous-people/james-
earl-jones?gclid=CjwKCAjw7e_oBRB7EiwAlH-
goNFusHyXoJdINAMJwhIpaenvO2XSTRdhO9RTTpotUR
xoHXKg-g-GDhoCIREQAvD_BwE

Weiss, D. C. (2011, Aug. 22). Study of Israeli Parole Board
Shows Why Good Scheduling Promotes Better Decisions.
ABA Journal. Retrieved from www.abajournal.com